Central America

Alyxx Meléndez

Consultants

Doris Namala, Ph.D.
Assistant Professor of History
Riverside City College

Esperanza Noriega
General Director
New Edulight, Mexico

Jon Anger
English, History, and ELD Teacher
Novato Unified School District

Publishing Credits

Rachelle Cracchiolo, M.S.Ed., *Publisher*
Emily R. Smith, M.A.Ed., *SVP of Content Development*
Véronique Bos, *Vice President of Creative*
Dani Neiley, *Editor*
Fabiola Sepulveda, *Series Graphic Designer*

Image Credits: p.10 © Look and Learn/Bridgeman Images; p.11 (top) Alamy/PhotoStock-Israel; p.12 Alamy/SeaTops; p.14 Luis Vergara Ahumada; p.15 Getty Images/Bettmann; p.16 (bottom) Alamy/Lucy Brown (loca4motion); p.16 (top) Getty Images/Kike Calvo; p.17 Alamy/Lena Schmidt; p.18 Getty Images/Bloomberg; p.19 (top) U.S. Embassy Belize; p19 (bottom) Getty Images/Ullstein Bild Dtl.; p.20 Alamy/Dennis Cox; p.21 (top) Carlos Sebastián; p.21 (bottom) Alamy/blickwinkel; p.24 (top) Alamy/Alpha Stock; p.26 (top) Alamy/Andrew Pearson; p.32 Newscom/Yonhap News/YNA; all other images from iStock and/or Shutterstock

Library of Congress Cataloging-in-Publication Data

Names: Melendez, Alyxx, author.
Title: Central America / Alyxx Melendez.
Description: Huntington Beach, CA : Teacher Created Materials, Inc, [2023] | Includes index. | Audience: Ages 8-18 | Summary: "Central America serves as a bridge between the Americas. It is a land formed by lava and shaped by the many living beings who call it home. The first people who lived there still influence its culture and politics today. Learn how different groups of people share their ways of life on this isthmus"-- Provided by publisher.
Identifiers: LCCN 2022038220 (print) | LCCN 2022038221 (ebook) | ISBN 9781087695105 (paperback) | ISBN 9781087695266 (ebook)
Subjects: LCSH: Central America--Juvenile literature.
Classification: LCC F1428.5 .M45 2023 (print) | LCC F1428.5 (ebook) | DDC 972.8--dc23/eng/20220810
LC record available at https://lccn.loc.gov/2022038220
LC ebook record available at https://lccn.loc.gov/2022038221

**Shown on the cover is Volcán San Pedro
in Guatemala.**

5482 Argosy Avenue
Huntington Beach, CA 92649
www.tcmpub.com
ISBN 978-1-0876-9510-5
© 2023 Teacher Created Materials, Inc.

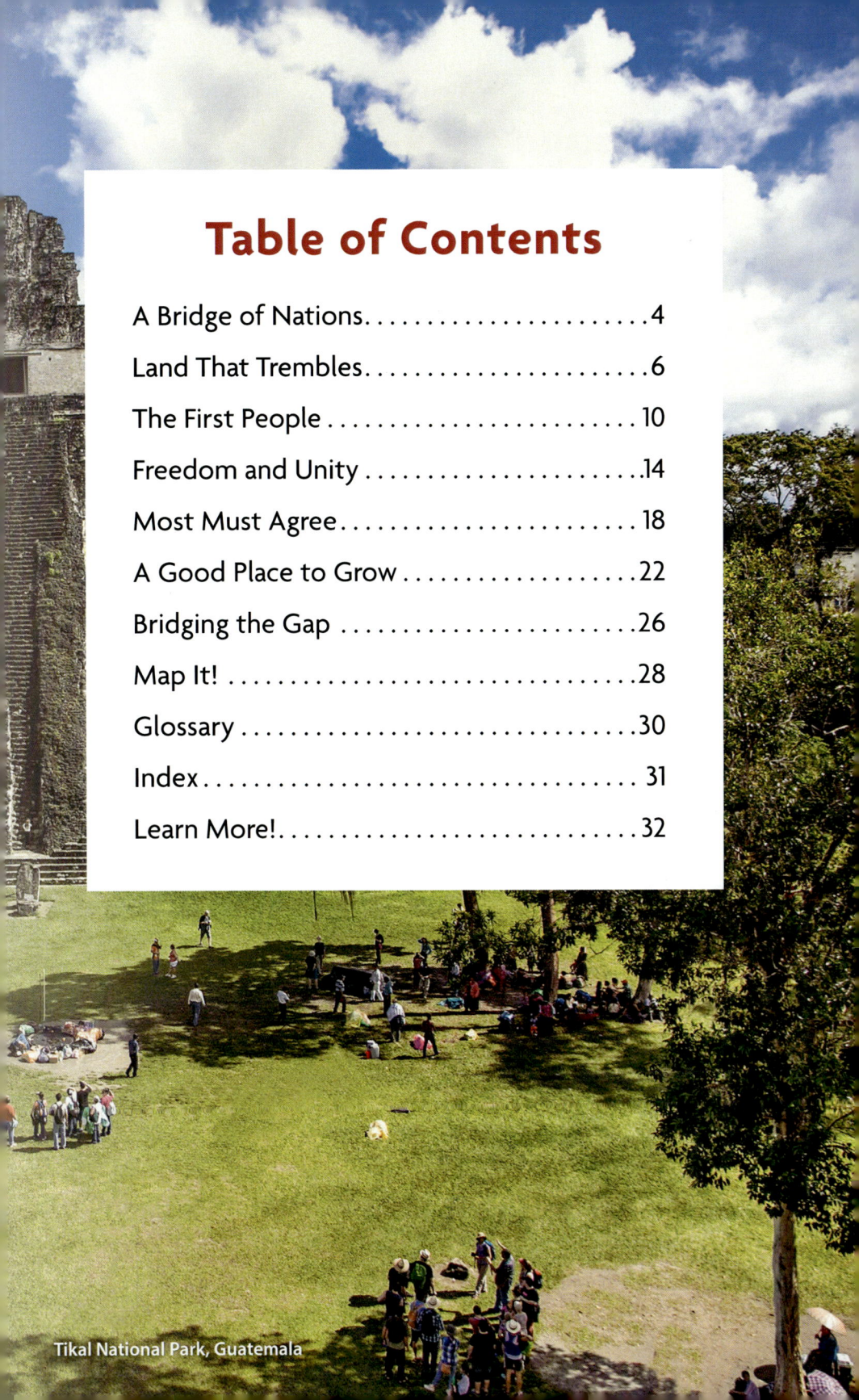

Table of Contents

Tikal National Park, Guatemala

A Bridge of Nations

North America and South America are connected by a thin strip of land. This land is called an **isthmus**. Seven countries make up this isthmus. Together, they are known as Central America. Belize and Guatemala lie at the north end. These two countries wrap around the edge of Mexico. Next, El Salvador and Honduras jut out to the northeast. Nicaragua lies to the south. Costa Rica follows. Panama is farthest south. This thin, curvy country touches the top of Colombia.

Central America has always been a **diverse** place. Wildlife and people from both North and South America meet there. Different languages are spoken in these countries. These include Spanish, English, and many **Indigenous** languages. Countless groups of animals and people **coexist** in this region. Central America is full of life!

island in Belize

Laguna de Alegria in El Salvador

4

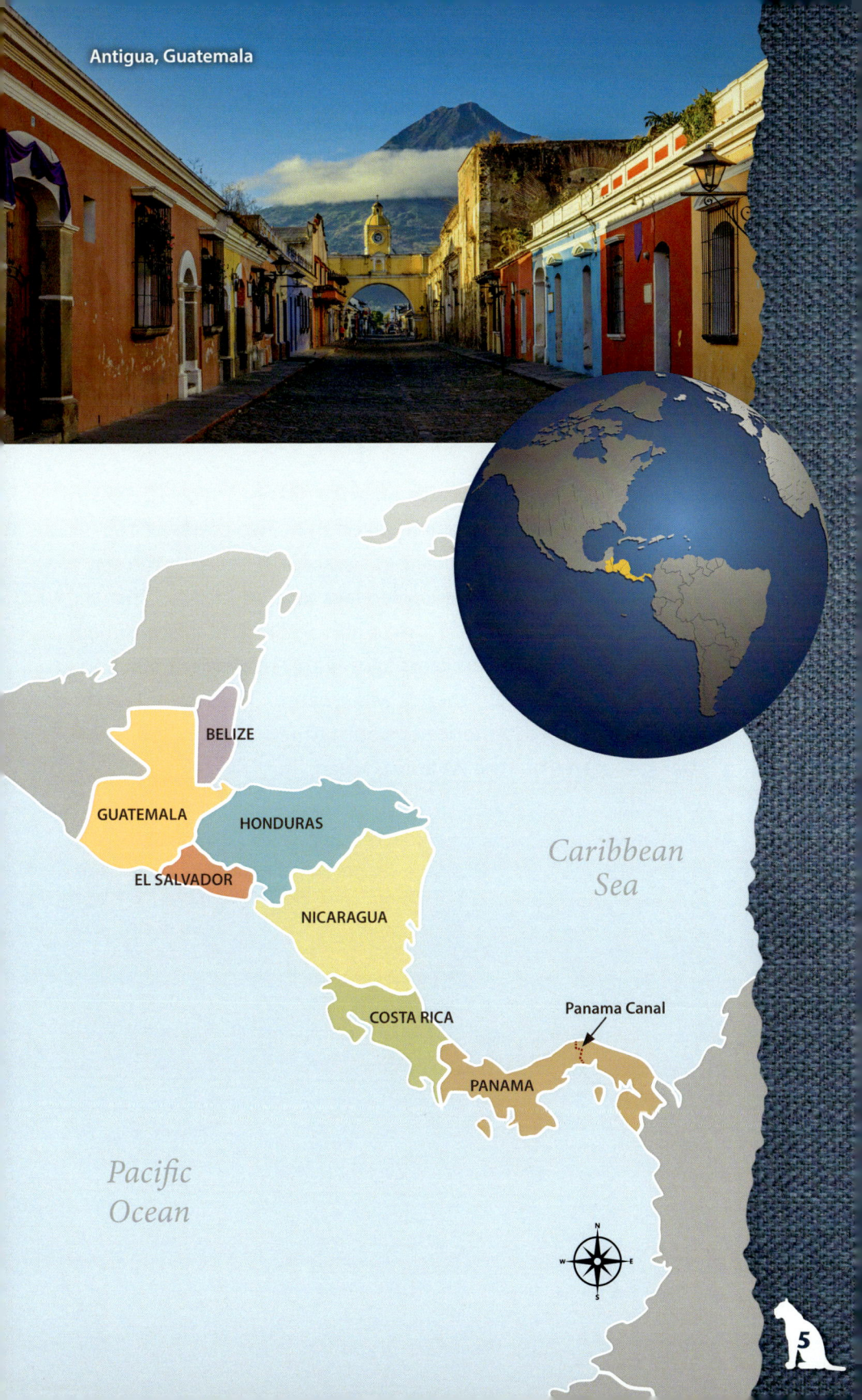

Antigua, Guatemala

BELIZE

GUATEMALA

HONDURAS

EL SALVADOR

NICARAGUA

Caribbean Sea

COSTA RICA

Panama Canal

PANAMA

Pacific Ocean

5

Land That Trembles

North America and South America did not touch 20 million years ago. Land movement changed this. Two plates of the earth's crust collided. Volcanoes burst forth beneath the sea. Shifting land and layers of cooled lava formed islands. The earth's crust collided and formed hills and mountains with high **elevation**. Three million years ago, all this movement resulted in a big change. Central America was created. The land served as a bridge from North America to South America. It also cut off the Pacific Ocean from the Atlantic Ocean.

two volcanoes in Guatemala

the island of Roatán in Honduras

La Fortuna Waterfall, Costa Rica

Central America's coasts are the flattest areas in the region. Wet, green swamps can be found past the beaches. Farther inland, lush forests blanket the rising mountains. Spruce, pine, and fir trees thrive on the dry Pacific side. Wetter air hydrates rain forests on the Atlantic side.

A chain of volcanoes runs along the center of the isthmus. Many volcanoes there are **dormant**, but several are active. The active volcanoes often spew gases and ash. They can also erupt with streams of hot lava. These eruptions can be good for the surrounding soil. Ash from volcanoes is full of nutrients. Volcanic soil is especially good for growing crops. Guatemala's volcanoes are the most active. And earthquakes are also common in this region. These events can be damaging. They may destroy homes and take lives.

North or South?

Central America touches North America and South America. But which continent is it part of? The line between the two continents is drawn at the southern border of Panama. This makes Central America a part of North America.

Hurricanes can intensify over the warm waters of the Gulf of Mexico.

Sky That Swirls

Weather all over the world changed when Central America formed. The new land bridge forced Atlantic Ocean currents to flow differently. Water headed north, which made the climate all the way in Europe much warmer. Ocean currents began to swirl in a pattern called the *Gulf Stream*. The twisting Gulf Stream made **tropical cyclone** winds much stronger.

Cyclones are part of life in Central America. On average, one hurricane hits the region each year. When a cyclone's winds spin more than 75 miles (120 kilometers) per hour, it becomes a hurricane. These strong storms can destroy cities and wildlife.

Tropical storms can cause flooding in communities.

The Gulf Stream makes Central America's climate very wet in the eastern region. Twice as much rain falls on the Atlantic side of the isthmus as the Pacific side. Rain falls most heavily from May to November. Most areas have a tropical climate. But this is not true for all of Central America. Weather can be very different from one country to the next. This happens because there are so many different types of land. The flat coasts and swamps are humid. High in the mountains, there is less water in the air. So, temperatures tend to be colder there.

forest in San José Pinula, Guatemala

Isla Tortuga, Costa Rica

Little but Lively

Central America takes up just 0.5 percent of the land on Earth. Despite its size, this small space is teeming with life! More than 7 percent of Earth's **biodiversity** can be found there.

The First People

Central America was, and still is, home to the Maya. They have lived in what is now Mexico and Guatemala since 1500 BCE. The Maya made great leaps in writing, math, and astronomy. They spoke several languages. They used **hieroglyphs** to write. These were pictures of real-life objects. The hieroglyphs represented animals, people, or other objects. The Maya also used logograms. These were pictures that represented single words.

Maya hieroglyphs

The Maya had a symbol to represent the number zero. Zero is needed to solve complex math problems. With zero, Maya priests made a set of three accurate calendars. The first calculated when to plant and harvest crops. The second planned religious ceremonies. The third calendar kept track of long stretches of time. The Maya built large pyramids and temples to honor their gods. They also built palaces for their rulers.

Music was an important part of Maya culture.

Indigenous peoples from Costa Rica

South of where the Maya lived, a different way of life prevailed. Most people there spoke Chibchan languages. These languages come from what is now Costa Rica and Panama. As people spread out through the isthmus, they changed how they spoke. Dozens of distinct languages formed. However, their cultures remained similar. Each group was made up of people with shared ancestors. They built small villages and created sculptures from clay, stone, and gold. Gold was often used in religious art.

Common Tongues

There were multiple Chibchan languages. People who spoke these different languages still needed to talk to each other. They had to communicate to trade goods. So, they had a lingua franca. This was a language that both speakers could understand. Sometimes, it was a blend of both speakers' languages. But it could also be its own separate language.

Conquest and Resistance

Settlers from Europe were a threat to Indigenous peoples. They threatened their ways of life. Spanish settlers spent the 16th century at war for new land. Spain claimed much of Central America. Great Britain claimed part of the east coast. Indigenous peoples fought to keep their land. European diseases quickly spread among them. More Indigenous peoples died from diseases than from battle wounds.

Still, Indigenous communities survived. They found ways to coexist. Some Indigenous survivors had children with Spanish settlers. This formed an ethnic group known as *mestizos*. This means "people of mixed descent." Indigenous peoples faced many pressures to become like Spanish settlers. The settlers forced groups to follow their way of life. Indigenous peoples faced **persecution**. Settlers even forced them to practice their religion in secret. But Indigenous peoples found ways to persist. This was especially true in areas that were farther away from Spanish settlements. Their traditions were more likely to survive in rural areas.

members of the Maleku tribe in Costa Rica

Garífuna performers in Belize

Children of Shipwreck

Two slave trading ships crashed in 1635. The West Africans on board escaped slavery. They hid with the Indigenous Carib people. Some West Africans and Caribs got married. Their descendants are known as the Garífuna.

Central America gave shelter to other people, too. Enslaved Africans escaped to the east coast. They built settlements where they could be free. The Garífuna are one example. They mostly settled in Honduras.

beach in the Caribbean

independence celebration in El Salvador

Freedom and Unity

The people of Central America and Mexico fought for independence. People did not want to be taxed by Europe. They wanted to make their own laws. They wanted to have their own governments. The people in these colonies wanted to be free. The first cry for independence broke out in El Salvador. In 1811, rebels rushed to its capital city. They made speeches in the town square. The rebels' beliefs spread far and wide. People in Nicaragua joined next. People in Guatemala, Honduras, and Costa Rica followed. Together, colonies in Mexico and Central America declared independence. They signed a document called the Act of Independence of the Mexican Empire. This happened in 1821.

However, political struggles continued in Mexico. So, Central America broke away. It declared itself the Federal Republic of Central America in 1824. This republic lasted for 17 years. But then, civil wars tore the union apart. The former colonies tried to unite three more times over the next 50 years. Two of these attempts lasted two years. The third lasted just one month.

The people of Panama took a different path. They broke free from Spain in 1821. Then, Panama joined a union called Gran Colombia. This union was based in South America. Panama did not govern itself for 80 more years.

The people of Belize took a different path, too. Belize was the only British colony in Central America. It was the last to be free. In the 20th century, its economy crashed. Many people lost their jobs. Great Britain did not do very much to help. This caused people to reject British rule. Belize gained independence in 1981.

the prime minister of Belize in 1981

Celebrating Independence Day

Independence took a long time in Central America. People were happy to be free. So, Independence Day became a national holiday. Each year, every country celebrates. People gather in town squares. Cities have parades. Some places have festivals.

Cultural Legacies

One **legacy** of Spanish rule in Central America is religion. More than four out of five people in the region are Catholic. Spanish settlers forced Indigenous peoples to follow this faith. Other people in the region are Protestant.

Central America is known for its blend of cultures. Dance styles reflect this blend. In the East, Garífuna people dance the *punta*. This dance has roots in African and Carib styles. In the North, people perform both Maya and Spanish folk dances. In the South, dancers move their hips to *cumbia*. This was first danced by enslaved Africans.

Cumbia dancers

Catholic procession in Guatemala

Scientific Progress

Many scientific advances have been made in Central America. These projects can help all life on Earth. In Guatemala, the Maya Achi people store their seeds in a seed bank. The bank stores crops that are native to their lands. It preserves the seeds. Since large farms only grow a few types of crops, all other crops may become extinct. Seed banks help farmers save and revive plant species.

People in Costa Rica launched the region's first satellite called *Irazú*. It launched in 2018. It measured the health of Costa Rican rain forests. *Irazú* kept track of the humidity, temperature, and carbon levels in the air. Its mission ended in 2020.

Farmers like this one in Guatemala rely on seeds to grow their crops.

Most Must Agree

In Central America, people take part in elections. They decide on the leaders who will run each nation. Elections work the same way in most countries in this region. Two or more candidates run against each other to be the next president. The candidates make speeches that tell how they plan to lead. The people vote for the candidate they want to win. Then, the president is elected by popular vote. That means the person who gets the most votes is the next president. In Costa Rica, all citizens over the age of 18 have to register to vote. They have to participate in elections. It is required. People wave bright flags to show their political views. Most citizens get time off from work to vote. That way, everyone's voices can be heard.

Costa Ricans show their support for a political candidate.

Froyla Tzalam, third governor-general of Belize

In Belize, elections are much different. This is because it was ruled by Great Britain, not Spain. Belize is led by two heads of government. They are called the prime minister and the governor-general. The people do not vote for these leaders like they would for a president. Instead, they vote to elect **legislators**. Belize's laws are made by its National Assembly. The National Assembly has 44 seats. The people vote to fill its 31 most powerful seats. The governor-general appoints the other 13 seats.

Violeta Chamorro

Leading Ladies

Belize's first governor-general was a woman named Elmira Minita Gordon. Her term lasted from 1981 to 1993. Violeta Chamorro was Central America's first female president. She led Nicaragua from 1990 to 1997.

All Must Agree

Countries in Central America are made up of different groups of people. Each group has their own way to make decisions. This can be seen in Central America's Indigenous peoples. Many of them have kept their ways of life alive for hundreds of years. The Maya have done this through language. Around 30 Maya languages can be heard in Central America. Not all Maya are the same. Still, they share similar traditions.

The Maya who follow traditional lifestyles often live in rural areas. A council of elders leads each group of Maya. To be an elder, a candidate must gain everyone's trust. They prove their worth by serving the community for many years. Then, they are elected through a **consensus**. If just one person thinks a candidate is not fit for the job, they will not become an elder. All parts of Maya life are shaped by their strong belief in consensus. The council of elders cannot act without a consensus. The community must agree with each of their decisions. This belief can also be seen in ancient Maya land ownership. A single person could not own land. Instead, the whole community owned the land. Together, they decided how to use it. Everyone shared farmland and meeting spaces.

Maya students at school in Honduras

Thelma Cabrera

Thelma Cabrera

Thelma Cabrera is an **advocate**. She fights for Indigenous peoples in Guatemala. Nearly 60 percent of the people in this country are Indigenous. In 2019, she ran for president. She was only the second Indigenous woman to do so. She lost the election. But Cabrera still continues to fight for rights and representation.

Maya leaders attend a ceremony in Guatemala.

cornfield in Guatemala

A Good Place to Grow

Rich soil has made Central America a prime spot to farm. Its Indigenous peoples were the first to learn this. They grew native crops, such as corn, beans, and squash. These foods sustained large Maya city-states in the North. Chibchan speakers in the South also relied on these foods. Then, colonial rule brought new crops and new demands. Some Spanish settlers began to own large sections of the land. Settlers also enslaved the Indigenous peoples who lived there. Settlers forced them to grow coffee and indigo. Most of the profits from the crops went to settlers who owned the land. The settlers barely paid Indigenous farm workers.

A man harvests coffee beans.

Flint corn is grown and harvested in Central America.

Before the 1900s, most farms in Central America were small. They did not produce large amounts of crops. Then, new technology changed farming worldwide. New machines could plant and harvest crops. They could do this faster than farmers. This meant Central American land owners could grow more crops. Land owners started to use the land for large cotton, sugar, and beef farms.

Today, these **plantations** can be found across the region. Guatemala, Honduras, and El Salvador are just a few of the countries that have large plantations. The soil across these countries is very fertile. And the climate is diverse across the land. Some places get more rain or more sun than others. This allows farmers to grow a wide variety of crops. A large amount of fruits, vegetables, flowers, and other plants are grown in the region and exported to other countries.

Why Not "Ecuador Hats"?

Panama hats are made from straw. They are meant to protect wearers from the sun. The name might make you think they are from Panama—but they aren't! Artisans in Ecuador wove them first. Then, they were exported to Panama starting in the mid-19th century.

Construction and Trade

Colonizers wanted to build a **canal** through Panama for centuries. This would allow for a shortcut between the Atlantic Ocean and the Pacific Ocean. With this in mind, the United States bought part of Panama in 1902. At the time, Panama was part of Colombia. Colombia did not agree to build a canal. Tensions were high. But still, the United States continued with their plan to build a canal. Troops from the United States and Panama took over the area. Workers from all around the world built the canal. They had to work in brutal, often deadly conditions.

The canal opened at last in 1914. For over 80 years, the United States owned the canal. This led to continued conflict with Panama. The United States gave up the rights to the canal in 1999.

Panama Canal construction in the 1900s

Panama Canal in 2017

the Inter-American Highway in Nicaragua

The United States also pushed to build a road. It was called the Inter-American Highway. It ran from Mexico to Panama. The idea for the road came about in 1923. The road was fully opened in the 1960s. Much of the road goes through **remote** areas.

Five countries signed a trade deal with the United States in 2005. This deal is called the Central America Free Trade Agreement (CAFTA). The Dominican Republic also joined this agreement. The agreement helped remove taxes on imports and exports. Before this agreement, countries had to pay high prices for certain goods. The agreement allowed the countries to trade and sell goods more easily. Coffee, bananas, and sugar became cheaper. More goods could be sold and bought, too.

Vacation Destination

Each day, tourists flock to the shores of Belize and Nicaragua. Costa Rica has also long been a popular place to visit. Resorts, tours, and all sorts of activities boost these nations' economies.

white water rafting in Costa Rica

Bridging the Gap

Two worlds **converge** in the isthmus between North America and South America. Plants, animals, and people from all around the world live there. They face volcanic eruptions and strong storms together.

Wildlife species need each other to survive. This is especially true for rain forests in Central America. Most of the region's biodiversity lies there. Mammals, such as Baird's tapirs and capybaras, feast on grasses and tree bark. Spotted jaguars hunt these mammals. Though they are killers, jaguars are essential to the ecosystem. Without them, their prey would be free to chew through the rain forest.

Baird's tapir

jaguar

a market in Santa María de Jesús, Guatemala

Many groups of Indigenous peoples lived in Central America first. Each group takes pride in their distinct cultures and ways of life. They lend their unique views to science, politics, and the arts. Their work in these fields often centers on protecting their traditions and the land they live on.

The seven countries of Central America are distinct. Each one has its own history. There is a wide range of land features across the region. Crops grown there are sold around the world. And people will continue to thrive in Central America, just as they have for thousands of years.

Herculean Strength

Honduras is home to the Hercules beetle. This big, brawny bug can be up to 7 inches (17.8 centimeters) long. Its pincers can lift 850 times its weight.

27

Map It!

Central America is full of high and low points. Flatlands and mountains exist there. Make a map that shows these different levels of elevation. Include a map key that lists the colors and elevations.

1. Draw a map of the outline of Central America. Draw in each country's border.

2. The coasts are the lowest points. They are 0 to 1,640 feet (500 meters) above sea level. Color the coasts green.

3. A thin band of slopes leads up to taller hills in the center of the region. They are 1,640 to 3,281 feet (500 to 1,000 meters) above sea level. Color the slopes yellow.

4. The region's center is a large swath of hills. They are 3,281 to 6,562 feet (1,000 to 2,000 meters) above sea level. Color the hills orange.

5. The highest points are in Guatemala and Costa Rica. A few high points also dot the center of Honduras. They are more than 6,562 feet (2,000 meters) above sea level. Color the mountains red.

6. **Bonus:** Coffee grows best where the air is slightly cool. Would coffee grow better in a green zone or a red zone? Explain your answer.

coffee farm in Honduras

Gulf of Mexico

Pacific Ocean

Caribbean Sea

Masaya Volcano, Nicaragua

Taboga Island, Panama

Glossary

advocate—a person who supports and fights for a cause

biodiversity—the existence of many different kinds of plants and animals in an environment

canal—a human-made waterway that allows boats or ships to pass

coexist—to live in peace with each other

consensus—agreement of opinion shared by all people in a group

converge—come together

diverse—made up of people or things that are different from one another

dormant—not active

elevation—the height of something above sea level

hieroglyphs—pictorial characters in a system of writing

Indigenous—from or native to a particular area

isthmus—narrow stretch of land that links two larger areas

legacy—what is remembered or has an impact on future generations

legislators—lawmakers

persecution—unfair treatment of people, especially because of race or religion

plantations—large areas where people work to grow crops

remote—far, out-of-the-way, or secluded from other things

spam—online messages that are not wanted

tropical cyclone—a storm with fast winds that forms in the tropics

Index

South Water Caye in Belize

Learn More!

The history of Central America is rich and diverse. Some Central American leaders today work to preserve their history for the future. One such leader has dedicated her life to protecting the Indigenous peoples of Guatemala. She is Rigoberta Menchú.

- Use the internet to research Menchú and her work. Record the most important things about the work she does. Note the awards and honors she has won.

- Think about how people today learn about Menchú's work. How is that different from leaders in the past? What does Menchú do to share her ideas and demand change?

- After you learn about Menchú, think about an issue you care about as much as she cares about the people of Guatemala. Create two to three social media posts to show how you would demand change around your cause.